Animals
of Australia

Teresa O'Brien

 Koala Books

I look like a bear,
but I am not a bear,
who am I?

Who am I,
with sharp claws
and prickly spines,
digging in the forest?

Who am I,
a giant bird
that cannot fly?

Which animals can you spot hiding in this picture?